THE LAST
QUIZ NIGHT
ON EARTH

T0352481

The Last Quiz Night on Earth received its world premiere
in a production by Box of Tricks Theatre Company at
The Welcome Inn, Salford, in association with The Lowry
on 11 February 2020, before embarking on a tour.

Photography © Alex Mead / Decoy Media

CAST

Kathy	Meriel Scholfield
Rav	Shaban Dar
Bobby	Chris Jack
Fran	Amy Drake

CREATIVE TEAM

Playwright	Alison Carr
Director	Hannah Tyrrell-Pinder
Designer	Katie Scott
Sound Designer	Chris James
Associate Producer	Max Emmerson
Production Manager	Alice Longson
Assistant Director	Kitty Ball
Press & PR	Bill Elms Associates Ltd.

CAST BIOGRAPHIES

MERIEL SCHOLFIELD (KATHY)

Meriel trained at RADA.

Her theatre credits include: *The Manchester Project* (Monkeywood Theatre Company, HOME Manchester, National Theatre); *Julius Caesar, A Midsummer Night's Dream* (Storyhouse Theatre, Chester); *By Far the Greatest Team* (Monkeywood Theatre Co, The Lowry); *Equivalent* (JB SHORTS, Manchester), various roles (Hull Truck Theatre); *Smoke* (HOME Manchester), *The Northern School, Bent, Architect* (Bradford Playhouse); *Kes* (Oldham Colliseum); *If I Were You, Rosencrantz and Guildenstern Are Dead, Larkin With Women* (Library Theatre, Manchester); *The Accrington Pals* (West Yorkshire Playhouse); *Behind The Scenes at the Museum* (York Theatre Royal); *St Musgrave's Dance* (The Old Vic, London).

She has appeared in all the major soaps over the years, with several episodes of *Coronation Street*, three series of *Last Tango in Halifax* – as school secretary Beverly – and a couple of stints in *Doctors*. She is frequently cast as a member of the medical profession including, psychiatrists, speech therapists and GPs, in shows ranging from *Hollyoaks* to *Casualty, The Royal, Courtroom* and *Holby City*.

Meriel also voices audio books and has done for the past nine years.

SHABAN DAR (RAV)

Shaban's theatre credits include: *I Believe In Unicorns* (Theatre Alibi); *One Little Word* (M6 Theatre, National Tour); *Crossing the Line* (M6 Theatre Company); *Peggin' Out* (Unheard Theatre); *Slink* (Lancaster Playwright Prize, Dukes Theatre, Tamasha); *Take Back: Our Girls* (Take Back Theatre); *50 Years* (Waterside Theatre Manchester); *Freaked Out* (53 Two); *Brink* (Royal Exchange, Manchester).

CHRIS JACK (BOBBY)

Chris' theatre credits include: *Beryl* (Octagon Theatre, Bolton); *Noughts and Crosses* (Pilot Theatre/Derby Theatre/ Coventry Belgrade); *The Secret Garden* (York Theatre Royal); *Brighton Rock* (York Theatre Royal/Pilot Theatre); *The Secret Garden* (Theatre by the Lake, Keswick); *Our Town* (Royal Exchange Theatre); *Treasure Island* (Lancaster Dukes Theatre); *The Biscuits* (Pilot – CBBC); *The Two Noble Kinsmen* (RSC); *The Rover* (RSC) *Unsung* (Liverpool Everyman/DADAFest); *By Far The Greatest Team* (Monkeywood Theatre/The Lowry); *The Funfair* (HOME); *Clybourne Park* (Liverpool Unity Theatre/Said and Done); *Hunger for Trade* (Royal Exchange Theatre); *Mugabeland* (The Lowry Studio); *After Black Roses* (Royal Exchange Theatre); *Gullivers Travels* (Dragonbreath Theatre/Leicester Curve Theatre); *Northern Soul* (The Royal Exchange Theatre); *A View From The Bridge* (The Royal Exchange Theatre).

Recent television credits include: *Emmerdale* (ITV); *Hollyoaks* (LIME Pictures); *Coronation Street* (ITV); *Creeped Out*, *The Dumping Ground* and *All At Sea* (CBBC); *Waterloo Road* (Shed Productions); *That Peter Thing* (Open Mike Productions).

AMY DRAKE (FRAN)

Amy's theatre credits include: *A Christmas Carol* (Theatr Clwyd); *Tinned Up* (Oldham Coliseum/MAP/53two); *My Mother Said I Never Should* (Theatre By The Lake); *Babushka* (Hard Graft Theatre); *Under The Market Roof* (Junction 8 Theatre); *Treasure Island* (Lancaster Dukes Theatre); *Shakers* (Deaf Dog Theatre); *The Naked Truth* (World On Stage); *We Are The Multitude* (24:7 Theatre Festival); *In My Bed* (24:7 Theatre Festival); *We're Going On A Bear Hunt* (Octagon Theatre Bolton)

Her television credits include: *Cold Feet* (Big Talk), *Hollyoaks* (Lime Pictures) and *Emmerdale* (ITV).

CREATIVE TEAM BIOGRAPHIES

ALISON CARR (PLAYWRIGHT)

Alison's theatre credits include: *Tuesday* (National Theatre Connections 2020); *The Way To Happiness* (Small Truth Theatre); *Caterpillar* (Theatre503/Stephen Joseph Theatre); *Hush* (Paines Plough/RWCMD/ Gate Theatre); *Remains* (troublehouse theatre, Octagon Theatre); *Iris* (Live Theatre, Winner – Writer of the Year, Journal Culture Awards); *Fat Alice* (Traverse Theatre/Oran Mor/Aberdeen Performing Arts); *The Soaking Of Vera Shrimp* (Winner, Live Theatre/The Empty Space Bursary Award); *A Wondrous Place* (Northern Spirit, Nominee - Best Studio Production, Manchester Theatre Awards); *Can Cause Death* starring Olivier Award-winning actor David Bradley (Forward Theatre Project - National Theatre/ Northern Stage/Latitude Festival).

Radio credits include *Dolly Would* (Afternoon Drama, BBC Radio 4) and *Yackety Yak* (The Verb, BBC Radio 3).

HANNAH TYRRELL-PINDER (JOINT ARTISTIC DIRECTOR & DIRECTOR)

Hannah trained as a director at Mountview Academy of Theatre Arts and is Joint Artistic Director of Box of Tricks. Directing credits for Box of Tricks include: *SparkPlug* (National Tour 2019) *Narvik* (Liverpool Playhouse Studio 2015 and national tour 2017); *In Doggerland* (national tour); Word:Play/NWxSW (Regional Tour); *Picture a City* (Everyword 2012, Liverpool Playhouse); *London Tales* (Waterloo East and Nu:Write Festival, Zagreb); *Head/Heart* (national tour); *Word:Play 4* (Arcola); *True Love Waits* (Latitude, Pulse, Nu:Write Festivals); *Word:Play 3* (Theatre 503); *Whispering Happiness* (Tristan Bates); *Captain of the School Football Team* (Hotbed and Latitude festivals '09); *Word:Play 2* (Theatre 503); *Word:Play* (Union Theatre); *A Hole in the Fence* and *Rural* (White Bear). Other directing includes: *Uprising* (Monkeywood at The Lowry); *JB Shorts 11* (Joshua Brooks) *Narvik* (Everyword 2013), *100 Seel St* (The Alligator Club, Liverpool), *JB Shorts 7* (Joshua Brooks). She is a script reader for The Royal Exchange, and the Bruntwood Playwriting Prize.

KATIE SCOTT (ASSOCIATE ARTIST: DESIGNER)

Katie is an award-winning Designer based in the North West. After graduating from LIPA in 2012, Katie was the inaugural recipient of the Liverpool Everyman & Playhouse Prize for Theatre Design. Katie was recently shortlisted to be a member of the Old Vic 12 and is an Associate Artist of Box Of Tricks Theatre Company. Design credits include: *Cinderella* (Dukes Theatre), *Seagulls* (Bolton Octagon in association with Middle Child), *Under Three Moons* (Box Of Tricks), *Peter Pan* (The Dukes Lancaster), *A Skull in Connemara* (Oldham Coliseum), *Narvik* (Box of Tricks Theatre Company - National Studio Tour- Winner of Best New Play UK Theatre Awards), *Plastic Figurines* (Box of Tricks Theatre Company – National Studio Tour), *Chip Shop Chips* (Box of Tricks Theatre Company – National Tour), *Under the Market Roof* (Junction8 Theatre Company), *Held* (Liverpool Playhouse Studio – Winner of Everyman & Playhouse Design Prize and Daily Post Arts Award for Best Design 2012).

CHRIS JAMES (ASSOCIATE ARTIST: SOUND DESIGNER)

Chris, who grew up in South Africa, has been surrounded by theatre his entire life. He followed his (self-proclaimed) 'master of all trades and jack of none' father's footsteps in entering the industry as a teenager before moving to the UK.

He worked as Head of Sound for the national tours of *Fame*, *Rock of Ages*, *Hairspray*, *Million Dollar Quartet*, *The King & I*, *Blood Brothers* and *Cabaret*. He worked as a Sound and Broadcast Supervisor at the Royal Opera House Muscat, in Oman, getting the opportunity to work some of the world's leading Opera, Ballet, Jazz and World Music artists.

He has been an associate artist with Box of Tricks Theatre Company for more than 10 years.

Sound Designs include: *Giraffes Can't Dance* (UK Tour), *The Entertainer* (UK Tour), *Bollywood Jane* (Leicester Curve), *Under Three Moons*, SparkPlug, *Chip Shop Chips*, *Plastic Figurines*, *In Doggerland*, *My Arms*, *Whispering Happiness*, *WordPlay*, *WordPlay2*, *A Hole in the Fence*, *Streetlights and Shadows*, *Rural*, and *Beyond Omarska* (Box of Tricks Theatre) *Romeo and Juliet* and *A Servant of Two Masters* (Michael Bogdanov's Wales Theatre Company)

Associate Sound Designs include: *The Nico Project* (Melbourne International Arts Festival), *The Wedding Singer* (South Korea) *Democracy* (Old Vic Theatre), *School for Scandal* (Bath Theatre Royal), *The Bargain* (Bath Theatre Royal and National Tour)

MAX EMMERSON (ASSOCIATE PRODUCER)

Max trained as an Arts Manager at the Liverpool Institute for Performing Arts (LIPA). He is currently Creative Producer for Emmerson & Ward and has worked as Interim Producer at the Oldham Coliseum, Assistant Producer for the Royal Exchange Theatre and Bill Kenwright Productions in London. Producing credits include: *The MP*, *Aunty Mandy & Me* by Rob Ward (Leicester Curve), *Sex/Crime* by Alexis Gregory (Soho Theatre), *Under Three Moons* by Daniel Kanaber (UK Tour), *Riot Act* by Alexis Gregory (UK Tour), *Don't Bother* by Broccan Tyzack-Carlin (Edinburgh Fringe Festival), *No Miracles Here* by The Letter Room (UK Tour) *Gypsy Queen* by Rob Ward (UK tour), *SparkPlug* by David Judge, (UK Tour), *The Tempest* (Royal Exchange Theatre), *The People Are Singing* by Lizzie Nunnery (Royal Exchange Theatre), *Adam & Eve & Steve* by Chandler Warren (Edinburgh Fringe Festival), *Shout! The Mod Musical* (Liverpool Royal Court Theatre).

Max was the first recipient of the Anthony Field Producer Prize at LIPA and completed the Stage One Producers apprenticeship scheme in London.

ALICE LONGSON – PRODUCTION MANAGER

Alice trained with a BA Hons in Media Performance from the University of Salford.

As Production Manager, Alice's credits include Stephen Sondheim's *Putting it Together* (Hope Mill Theatre), *Rags* (Hope Mill Theatre), *Catching Comets* (Ransack Theatre Productions).

Alice's Stage Manager credits include *The Trial* (People Zoo Productions), *A Kidnapping* (Swaggering Crow Productions), *Moth* (Ransack Theatre Productions), *The Party's Over* (Nonsuch Theatre), *Edward Gant and* His *Amazing Feats of Loneliness* (People Zoo Productions), *Be//Longing* (Take Back Theatre), *Bear and Butterfly* UK Tour (Hullabaloo Theatre Company), *Jesus Hopped the A Train* (Ellysium Theatre Company), *Catching Comets* (Ransack Theatre Productions) and *I Wanna Be Yours* UK Tour (Paines Plough).

KITTY BALL – ASSISTANT DIRECTOR

Kitty was on placement for *The Last Quiz Night on Earth* from the MA Theatre Directing Course at The Academy of Live and Recorded Arts, North. She was selected to be a Northern Creative 2019 in conjunction with Arts Council England and BBC Arts, commissioned to write an audio piece for BBC Sounds called '*Another Joan*'.

Kitty's Assistant Director credits include *The Jungle Book* (Oldham Coliseum 2020), *Treasure Island* (ALRA North 2019) and *Lancastrians* (Junction 8 Theatre).

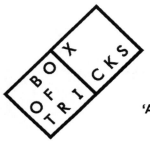

The play makers

'A theatre company to watch'
The Stage

Box of Tricks makes plays. We champion playwrights and empower them to tell the stories they want to tell. Together, we go on a journey to uncover new plays that reflect the world in which we live today. We create heartfelt theatre that resonates, inspires and entertains.

New plays are the lifeblood of theatre, and playwrights its beating heart. Box of Tricks nurtures the next generation through our year-long PlayBox attachments for early-career playwrights. We commission, develop and produce bold new theatre from the most exciting voices through our New Tricks commissioning programme.

Box of Tricks brings people together to share stories collectively. Based in Manchester, we engage audiences far and wide. We stage productions in theatres right across the UK and in public spaces – pubs, libraries, village halls – in the heart of local communities.

Our engagement programme goes beyond productions. We provide pathways into the arts, connect with communities, inspire younger generations and develop future talent.

We are the play makers. Every story told. Every voice heard.

Box of Tricks is an Associate Company at Stephen Joseph Theatre, Scarborough.

Recent productions include: *Under Three Moons* by Daniel Kanaber (National Tour), *SparkPlug* by David Judge (National Tour), *Chip Shop Chips* by Becky Prestwich (Northern and National Tours), *Narvik* by Lizzie Nunnery (National Tour) and *Plastic Figurines* by Ella Carmen Greenhill (National Tour).

Joint Artistic Directors	Hannah Tyrrell-Pinder
	Adam Quayle
Associate Producer	Max Emmerson
Audience	
& Marketing Associate	Al Lockhart-Morley
Artistic Associates	Chris Hope
	Chris James
	Katie Scott
	Richard Owen

boxoftrickstheatre.co.uk

THANK YOU TO

Our Playmaker Patrons (Sue Tyrrell, John and Gloria
Quayle, Kath Quick and Ed Benson); our Board (Caz
Brader, David Bryan, Rhiannon McKay Smith, John
Quayle); Forge Dynamic; Hannah Ellis at Play with Fire
Productions; Kirsty Barlow and the Bolton Octagon,
Oldham Coliseum and ALRA North.

SUPPORTED BY

Arts Council England
The Granada Foundation
The Unity Theatre Fund

Supported using public funding by
**ARTS COUNCIL
ENGLAND**

THE LAST QUIZ NIGHT ON EARTH

Alison Carr

Characters

KATHY, *forties, pub landlady*
RAV, *twenties, bar man and quiz master*
BOBBY, *forties, Kathy's brother*
FRAN, *twenties, Rav's childhood sweetheart*

Kathy and Rav behave like they know the audience members as pub regulars. They call them by name (names I've made up for them) and interact with them as friends.

Location

The Four Horsemen pub.

Time

Right now. It all plays out in real time.

The Quiz

While quiz questions and answers are provided here, there can be flexibility around the delivery of the quiz – how often questions/answers are repeated, etc. It's a real quiz that the audience must be able to play properly. If you're performing this production and wish to edit or update the quiz questions, please do so. Though, obviously some need particular answers for reasons that are revealed at the end. The quiz for the original production was different to the one in this published edition.

This text went to press before the end of rehearsals and so may differ slightly from the play as performed.

Pre-set on the tables are quiz answer-sheets, printed with Rounds One to Five and spaces for six answers per round. There should also be space for a team name, and areas to tot up the scores. Also pens.

ACT ONE

An automated radio broadcast is playing on an old portable CD/radio/cassette player that is on the bar.

The broadcast is full of static but we catch key words. It repeats over and over as the audience come in.

VOICE. This is an Emergency Broadcast. This is an Emergency Broadcast. This is not a test. This is not a test. An asteroid is on a collision course with Earth, impact imminent. NASA have confirmed that all attempts to destroy or divert the object have failed. This is a World-Ending Event. Repeat, this is a World-Ending Event. This is not a test. Recommended action… thoughts and prayers.

KATHY greets the audience like friends and neighbours as they're coming in. Things like –

KATHY. Hi!

Good to see you.

Tom, Anna, great to see you.

Alright, Mags?

Hi. Hello.

Dannyyyyyy.

Come in, please, make yourselves comfortable.

Gerry, your favourite table's there waiting. No one would dare.

Etc, etc.

Once everyone is largely settled, KATHY *gets things going –*

Right, let's turn this blather off. What more can they say, eh?

She turns the broadcast off.

That's better.

So. First things first – thank you, thank you from the bottom of my heart for choosing to spend your last night here with us at the Horsemen. It means so much, it really, really does.

Looking around – most of you I know, friends and neighbours...

Terry, is that your Susan you're always telling us about? Lovely to meet you at last, love. I wish it was under different circumstances but better late than never, eh. Or better late than pregnant, as my Aunt Viv always said.

Mary, no Chris? Decided to try and get down to see her Pat, did she? I can understand that and good luck to her.

Tasha. Andy. Naz.

Paul. (*Curt. A look, a history.*)

And those of you I don't know, and there are a few unfamiliar faces, welcome. I'm so pleased you found us, however you did. You're all welcome. Even Paul.

I'm so glad that we're all here together tonight...

She breaks off, emotional.

Sorry. Sorry.

That won't get me anywhere, will it? I'm sure we've all cried rivers these last few days. Raged, ranted, turned the air blue. But here we are. And there *it* is – (*Points to the heavens.*) and it's not stopping its trajectory while I stand here blubbing, so no more of that. (*Wipes her eyes, enough.*)

Now, Rav's just putting his distinctive finishing touches to the quiz and then we'll be off.

Really, we just want to keep everything as normal as possible.

We'll be keeping the telly off, and the radio. That might seem a bit – to some of you, but really what's the point in hearing a countdown to it all?

And the fact that you've chosen to come here, with us, to do the quiz, well, I think we're all on the same page.

Now, Rav's asked me to do some housekeeping –

Phones. I mean, the internet crashed hours ago so the chances of you being able to google the answers is virtually non-existent but he insisted I remind you: no cheating.

And the phone networks have been down all day, but if someone does get a message through or you get any signal, feel free to take a look but don't take the mick.

And, the bar won't be serving during the quiz. You know how he gets.

And yes, before you ask, we are still charging normal prices for all drinks and snacks. I'm a businesswoman to the end – I am my father's daughter, after all. If all this proves to be a big mistake – fingers crossed, eh – I'll still have bills to pay tomorrow. And if it's not, well, what are you going to do with that money burning a hole in your pocket? You can't take it with you.

RAV *sticks his head out.*

RAV. I'm ready.

KATHY. Oooh, he's ready, everybody.

Ladies and gentlemen, boys and –

RAV. Hang on. I need music.

Take this. (*Passes her a CD case.*) Track two.

KATHY *puts the CD in the player.*

Europe's 'The Final Countdown' plays.

KATHY. Ladies and gentlemen –

RAV. Don't talk over the beginning.

KATHY. What?

RAV (*re: the music*). Stop it.

She stops the track.

The beginning's the best bit.

KATHY. Sorry.

RAV. Start my intro after the beginning.

KATHY. When they start singing?

RAV. No. There's a moment, a change in the music – you'll hear it.

KATHY. What if I don't?

RAV. You will.

KATHY. But if I don't?

RAV. I'll give you a thumbs up when it's time to start.

Play it nice and loud. Okay?

KATHY. Okay.

RAV disappears again.

The song starts up again.

RAV (*off*). Louder.

KATHY turns it up.

It's a long intro with various points that COULD be the change in the music RAV referred to. There are some false starts but eventually RAV gives KATHY the thumbs up.

KATHY. Ladies and gentlemen, boys and girls, please welcome to the floor the one, the only, the irreplaceable, the incandescent, the irrrrr-itating as hell demanding this build-up every single time – I give you – RAV!

RAV enters in a sparkly jacket. He struts around believing the hype.

The CD starts to stick. KATHY stops it, takes it out of the player and gives it a wipe.

RAV. Well, that's ruined it.

KATHY. I'm amazed it works at all. It's ancient.

RAV. Your spare room's like going back in time.

That stereo.

This CD.

KATHY. These are classics, all.

RAV. If by 'classic' you mean 'old', there's certainly nothing after I was born.

KATHY *returns the CD to the player.*

KATHY. Do you want me to start the track again?

RAV. No. The moment's gone.

Sorry about that, everyone. Technical difficulties. It happens to the best of us.

But thank you, thank you for that warm... lukewarm... for that tepid reception.

Yes it's me, Rav, your quiz host with the most... difficult questions in town.

And tonight it's my end-of-the-world special. Never to be repeated. But there might be a little surprise at the end. We live in hope, eh.

So without further ado-do – let's get quizzical, quizzical, I wanna get quizzicaaaal...

He starts another track – it's the wrong one.

No, sorry. One sec –

How do I – ?

KATHY. Let me see. (*Takes charge of the stereo.*)

Which track do you want?

RAV. Number seven.

Elvis Costello's 'Waiting for the End of the World' plays as RAV explains the set-up.

There are answer sheets on your tables.

If you've come as a team, great.

If you want to buddy up with your table, also great. We're all friends here.

And if you're strangers, you're just friends who haven't met yet.

And if you don't get on, we'll all be dead soon so what does it matter?

There's a prize for the Best Team Name. One hundred pounds –

KATHY. What? I'm not stumping up a hundred pounds.

RAV. You probably won't have to. We'll all be dead soon.

KATHY. Yeah, I don't really want that to become tonight's catchphrase.

RAV. You know what, five hundred pounds for the Best Team Name.

KATHY. Rav!

RAV. What? We'll all be… (*Does he try to get the audience to join in?*) dead soon!

KATHY. You better hope this asteroid doesn't miss.

It better bloody land on your head.

RAV. Has everyone got everything? Hands up if you still need an answer sheet or a pen.

KATHY *can hand some more answer sheets and pens around if needed.*

Okay?

KATHY. I think so.

RAV. Great.

KATHY. Have you got a spare answer sheet? I've given mine away.

RAV. You hate my quizzes.

KATHY. I don't.

RAV. You say they're too hard.

KATHY. No, I say they're too obscure.

I hope this one's for everyone? We all want to be able to join in, have fun. That's the point.

RAV. Honestly, I think it's my best one ever.

KATHY. Why does that make me nervous?

RAV *hands* KATHY *a sheet and a pen. She sits at a table of her own at the front.*

RAV. Okay, everybody ready? Great.

Alright, Paul, I'm surprised to see you.

I thought he was barred?

KATHY. Like you say, we'll all be dead soon so what does it matter.

RAV. True.

(*Re: the CD player.*) Knock that off, will you, Kathy.

KATHY. What did your last slave die of? (*But she does.*)

RAV. He got hit by an asteroid.

Okay, let's go. Round One – General Knowledge.

QUESTION ONE. According to ABBA, my my, at – *where* – Napoleon did surrender?

KATHY. I know that one.

RAV. QUESTION TWO. Which sign of the zodiac is represented by a lion?

KATHY. And that one.

RAV. QUESTION THREE. Who did Barack Obama defeat to win the 2012 US Presidential election?

(*To* KATHY.) Do you know that one?

KATHY. Yes. (*She doesn't.*)

RAV. Next question. QUESTION FOUR. Globophobia is a fear of what?

QUESTION FIVE. In which decade was the first mobile phone call made?

QUESTION SIX. Last question in this round. 'Everyone I Have Ever Slept With 1963–1995' is a work by British artist Tracey who?

Okay, everyone got those?

Anyone need anything repeated?

Right, now if you can all swap sheets with a table nearby to be marked and we'll do the answers.

One point per correct answer. No half-points, I'm not messing about here.

My answer is the law, no debating. I'm looking at you, Shirl. I usually enjoy a healthy debate, but not tonight. Life's too short. Literally.

KATHY *(to a nearby table)*. Can I swap with you?

I'm a team of one here, so don't judge.

And actually, you lot, you've got an advantage cos, Sunny – you were on *Family Fortunes* back in the day, weren't you? Although –

'Name something made of wool.'

And you said?

AUDIENCE MEMBER *answers*.

You said 'sheep', Sunny. We all saw it.

And before anyone accuses me of cheating. This is a totally new quiz that Rav's put together for tonight –

RAV. Bespoke.

KATHY. Bespoke. So I've not heard any of these questions before.

BOBBY *crashes in – he's sweating and out of breath.*

Who's that? If that's looters –

What the hell are you doing here?

BOBBY. I need to …

KATHY. What?

BOBBY. I… (*But* BOBBY *can't speak yet.*)

RAV. Here, do you want to sit down?

BOBBY *shakes his head.*

KATHY. What's wrong with you?

BOBBY. I… all the way from… I… (*Mimes walking.*)

KATHY. You walked?

RAV. I'll get you a glass of water.

RAV *does.*

BOBBY *composes himself.*

BOBBY. I set off after the lunchtime bulletin.

KATHY. You've been walking for seven hours?

BOBBY. I ran the last bit.

That was a mistake.

KATHY. Clearly.

BOBBY. I tried driving but I barely got to the end of my street.
The roads are gridlocked.

RAV *returns with a glass of water.*

RAV. Here you go.

BOBBY *gulps it down fast.*

Slow down, you'll make yourself sick.

Another?

BOBBY. No.

(*To* KATHY.) We need to go.

KATHY. Go where?

BOBBY. Anywhere. Away from here.

KATHY. Why?

BOBBY. Oh, I don't know, maybe the massive asteroid heading
our way.

KATHY. Exactly.

BOBBY. Exactly.

KATHY. They're saying it's bigger than Singapore and it's
heading right for us.

Where's my Punto going to take us that can outrun that?

BOBBY. We have to try.

KATHY. No, we don't.

We can sit here, with friends, warm and safe, and we can do
a quiz.

BOBBY. A quiz?

RAV. A really good, bespoke quiz.

KATHY. That's how I want to go out.

BOBBY. Seriously?

KATHY. Yeah.

BOBBY. Seriously?

KATHY. Yes.

BOBBY. I don't believe this.

KATHY. What did you expect?

BOBBY. Look, Kathy, it's me, okay. You don't have to pretend.

KATHY. What do you mean?

BOBBY. Put on a brave face.

KATHY. I'm not.

BOBBY. Right, we haven't got time for this.

Come on. Come on.

He tries to grab her, pull her, force her to leave.

KATHY. Get off. Get off.

RAV. Oi.

KATHY pushes BOBBY away, hard.

KATHY. I'm not going anywhere.

I'm exactly where I want to be.

BOBBY. Seriously?

KATHY. Yes. How many times?

He blinks at her. She's resolute.

BOBBY. Can I take your car?

KATHY. Impact is due in – what? – two hours?

Where are you going to get to in that time?

BOBBY. Anywhere.

KATHY. You want to be sitting in a car – a disgusting car by the way, it's a hovel.

You want to be sitting on your own in a traffic jam going nowhere for your final moments?

BOBBY. Yes.

KATHY. Why?

BOBBY. Because it's not here.

KATHY (*frustrated*). You *came* here.

Christ alive, nothing changes, does it. You're still… (*Deep breath.*)

No. I'm not rising to it. Not tonight.

Here, look, have my car keys.

Go where you like, where you can.

BOBBY. That's it?

KATHY. I don't know what you want from me.

BOBBY. Fine.

KATHY. Fine.

BOBBY. Fine.

BOBBY goes.

RAV. Are you okay?

KATHY. Not really.

RAV. Is he an ex?

Kind of romantic of him to come to try and 'save' you.

That's chivalry, Paul, watch and learn.

KATHY. Bobby's my brother.

RAV. Oh.

I didn't know you had a brother.

KATHY. Well, I do. And that's him.

RAV. Where's he walked from? He was quite a state.

KATHY. No idea.

RAV. You don't know where he lives?

KATHY. No.

I haven't seen or spoken to him in twenty years.

She's staring at the place BOBBY *was standing.*

RAV. You could still catch up with him.

KATHY. When we were kids, for the whole Easter holidays one year, he echoed the last word of everything I said.

Can you imagine how annoying that is? All day, every day.

RAV. Day.

KATHY. Stop it.

RAV. It.

KATHY. I'm not joking.

RAV. Joking.

KATHY. I mean it.

RAV. It.

KATHY. Stop.

Have you stopped?

RAV. Yes.

KATHY. In the end –

RAV. End.

Sorry, sorry. I've stopped. Honestly.

KATHY. In the end I stopped talking altogether so he couldn't do it.

Eventually when I did venture to say something I waited for the echo and he just looked at me, smirking, like 'what?'.

I wanted to punch him then like I wanted to punch him just now.

That'll be my overriding memory of my brother – just wanting to lamp him one in his stupid face.

RAV. Well, if the predictions are right and the blast impact is bigger than an atomic bomb, he'll have no face left by 10 p.m.

KATHY. Don't say that.

RAV. Sorry.

KATHY. All of this was meant to be his, you know.

RAV. 'Everything the light touches.'

KATHY. But he didn't want it. Couldn't get away quick enough.

Devastated Dad.

Mum was thrilled. She wanted more for him.

RAV. But not for you?

KATHY. This place is all I ever wanted.

I came out the womb pulling a pint.

RAV. Sounds painful for your mum.

KATHY. He was going to sell up, Dad, when he got ill. I had to fight him not to.

He never once came in for a drink after I took over. None of them did.

RAV. That's shitty.

KATHY. Yeah.

RAV. Bobby's come in now, though. Better late than never?

KATHY. Yeah, to get me to leave. So he still doesn't get it.

I just wish that…

I've reached out to him time and time again…

Just because *he* decides…

Oh bloody hell…

She goes after BOBBY.

(*Leaving*.) Bobby. Bobby.

RAV (*calling after her*). You're the bigger person, Kathy.

Oooh, it's all happening tonight. A long-lost brother, eh. Who knew?

Right then, everyone, we'd better crack on. Answers to Round One.

One point per correct answer, remember.

ANSWER ONE. My, my at *Waterloo* Napoleon did surrender.

ANSWER TWO. The zodiac sign for *Leo* is a lion.

ANSWER THREE. –

KATHY *returns*.

KATHY. I missed him. He's gone.

RAV. Shit. I'm sorry.

KATHY. Sod him.

RAV. Sod him.

KATHY. I tried, you know.

RAV. You did.

KATHY. And a captain doesn't leave a sinking ship.

RAV. A queen doesn't leave her kingdom.

KATHY. I'm a queen and this is my kingdom?

RAV. Of course.

KATHY. Not a tyrant?

RAV. A benevolent dictator.

KATHY. I'll take that. Thank you.

> Come on then, Quiz Master General. We're all on tenderhooks here.

RAV. Tenter.

KATHY. What?

RAV. It's tenterhooks not tender.

KATHY. What's a 'tenter'?

RAV. No idea, but that's what it is.

KATHY. Are you sure?

RAV. Positive.

KATHY. Well, it's never too late to learn something.

RAV. From the top then, ladies and gents.

> And if the team you're marking for have got it wrong, please do a nice big cross and write the correct answer alongside it so we're all learning something new tonight.

> ANSWER ONE. My, my at *Waterloo* Napoleon did surrender.

> ANSWER TWO. The zodiac sign for *Leo* is a lion.

> ANSWER THREE. Barack Obama defeated *Mitt Romney* in the 2012 US Presidential election.

> ANSWER FOUR. Globophobics are afraid of *balloons*.

> ANSWER FIVE. The first mobile phone call was made in the *1970s*.

ANSWER SIX. Last answer in this round. Tracey *Emin* is the British artist.

Okay, and if you want to tot up those scores and swap your sheets back, we'll move swiftly on to Round Two – Sport.

KATHY (*groaning*). Really? Politics. I know Politics. Or flags.

RAV. Flags?

KATHY. Flags of the world. Show me any flag, I'll know it.

RAV. Round Two. Sport.

CD player – Queen's 'We Are The Champions' plays .

We can all enjoy that for a bit while the teams swap their sheets back and until RAV *is ready.*

Kathy, if you would, please.

KATHY *turns the CD off.*

Everybody ready?

KATHY. No.

RAV. They're easy. If you know the answers.

QUESTION ONE. Which British city hosted the 1970 Commonwealth Games?

QUESTION TWO. Who was the first woman to beat a man at the PDC Darts World Championship?

QUESTION THREE. What is the heaviest weight category in boxing?

QUESTION FOUR. Which is bigger, a full-sized football or a full-sized volleyball?

QUESTION FIVE. Who beat Roger Federer to win a gold medal at the 2012 Olympic men's single final at Wimbledon?

QUESTION SIX. Last question in this round. Two throwing events in track and field require safety netting. Discus and what else?

Okay, anyone need any repeating?

Right then. Swap sheets please.

KATHY. Rav.

RAV. Sorry, no clues, no special treatment.

KATHY. No, not that.

What I said before to Bobby, I really am exactly where I want to be.

RAV. I know that.

KATHY. You, though. Cos, sitting here looking at you just now, you're so young and –

RAV. And handsome.

KATHY. And handsome. That's a given, clearly. But, I really thought you'd go with the others.

RAV. You want shot of me? Charming.

KATHY. No, not at all. But I thought you'd at least try to get away.

RAV. We can't outrun it, you said so yourself.

KATHY. I know, but.

RAV. The quiz is something that I can *do*. Something practical. And I *want* to do it, truly. To bring some joy.

FRAN *bursts in*.

FRAN. Rav? Is Rav here?

RAV. What's this? My fanclub's arrived?

FRAN. Rav!

RAV. You alright, love?

FRAN. It's me.

RAV. So I see.

FRAN. I... I can't believe it's you.

RAV. The one and only.

FRAN. You haven't changed a bit.

KATHY. Do you want to introduce us to your friend?

RAV. I would if I could.

FRAN. What?

RAV. I'm sorry, I'm usually pretty good with faces but…

FRAN. It's me.

Me.

It's ME.

RAV, *uncomfortable, sings the refrain from Kate Bush's 'Wuthering Heights'.*

KATHY. Stop it.

You think you know Rav, love?

FRAN. I know I do.

KATHY. Okay. Where from?

FRAN. Before.

KATHY. From before? Before what?

FRAN. Before it all went wrong. (*Cries.*)

KATHY. There now, you're alright.

Are you sure you don't know her?

RAV. I don't think so.

What's her name?

KATHY. What's your name?

FRAN (*looking to* RAV). You really don't know?

RAV. I'm sorry.

FRAN. Fran.

KATHY. Pam?

FRAN. Fran.

KATHY (*to* RAV). Fran?

FRAN. Hillside Comp.

RAV. Bloody hell.

Fran. Francesca Burt.

FRAN. Burr. Francesca Burr.

RAV. We went to school together.

FRAN. We went out.

RAV. My God, look at you. All grown up.

FRAN. I think I'm going to throw up.

KATHY. What?

FRAN. Sorry, but –

KATHY. The toilet's through there.

FRAN *exits*.

Blimey.

RAV. Yeah.

What's she doing here?

KATHY. Dunno.

How long since you've seen her?

RAV. Ten years, give or take.

KATHY. Blast from the past, eh.

RAV. I'll say.

KATHY. It's going to be that kind of night.

RAV. Yeah.

KATHY. You went out together?

RAV. Yeah. For a bit.

Do you mind if I step out for a minute? I need some air.

KATHY. By 'air' do you mean 'cigarette'?

I thought you'd given up?

RAV. What does it matter now?

KATHY. Are you alright?

RAV. Yeah, just, when some woman you haven't seen since you were a teenager comes bowling in like a whirlwind – starts crying then vomits. It's just a bit, you know… on top of everything else.

KATHY. When you put it like that.

Go on, I'll do the answers to that last round.

RAV. Yeah?

Don't cheat.

KATHY. I've already given them my sheet.

RAV. Okay.

Keep an eye on that table too, they look shifty. Watch them.

KATHY. Like a hawk.

RAV *gives her the answer sheet and exits.*

KATHY *will also need to retrieve the sheet for the team she is marking for and mark it as she goes.*

Okay, right then, everyone.

Well, looking at this I think I got them all wrong.

Ready?

ANSWER ONE. Edinburgh.

ANSWER TWO. Fallon Sherrock.

ANSWER THREE. Super heavyweight.

ANSWER FOUR. A football.

ANSWER FIVE. Andy Murray.

ANSWER SIX. Hammer.

All got that? Anyone need any repeating?

(*To the team who has her sheet.*) How did I do?

AUDIENCE MEMBER *tells her score which is poor.*

Yeah? More than I was expecting.

So, if you can all tally those scores up and everyone swap back.

Everyone does as instructed.

Rav won't be long, then we'll crack on to Round Three.

Let's put some music on, eh. While we wait.

She scans the CD track list.

This one, going out to my brother Bobby.

The Proclaimers' 'I'm Gonna Be (500 Miles)' plays.

Enter FRAN.

Here she is. Feeling better?

FRAN. I wasn't sick.

KATHY. Good.

FRAN. I hate being sick.

KATHY. Me too.

FRAN. I should have known I wasn't going to actually be sick because my legs weren't shaking.

KATHY. Right.

FRAN. Do yours shake?

KATHY. Not that I've noticed.

FRAN. Mine do. If I'm going to be sick.

Then, though, just now, I was so het up that they might as well have been shaking but I didn't realise and I really thought I was going to be sick but then I wasn't sick.

KATHY. Can you stop saying 'sick' it's making me feel, well, sick.

FRAN. Sorry.

What must you think of me?

KATHY. I don't think anything, love.

FRAN. Course you do. Bursting in here, blathering on, being sick.

KATHY. But you weren't sick.

FRAN. No.

This isn't me, though. I don't do things like this.

KATHY. I think all bets are off at the moment, don't you?

Last night on Earth, nothing's normal.

FRAN. This looks pretty normal. In the pub, having a drink.

KATHY. It's all churning away, though, isn't it?

Inside. Underneath.

FRAN. I just assumed it would miss. They said they could knock it off-course. That scientist who kept coming on the news, she promised.

KATHY. You learn in this game, words are meaningless – it's people's eyes telling the truth, not what they say. And her eyes got more and more scared. Defeated.

FRAN. Where were you this morning, when the announcement came?

KATHY. Here.

FRAN. I was at work. It came up on everyone's computer. I thought we'd been hacked at first.

KATHY. I thought Claudia Winkleman was a good choice. If you'd asked me which celebrity I'd choose to present an emergency broadcast announcing the end of the world, she wouldn't have been my first choice –

FRAN. Nor me.

KATHY. But she made a good fist of it.

FRAN. She did.

KATHY. She's got lovely hair.

FRAN. Hasn't she, though?

Head and Shoulders.

KATHY. Really?

FRAN. Yeah.

When the video ended I don't think any of us were even breathing. Then bam – chaos. People crying, running out. Pushing and shoving.

KATHY. Including you?

FRAN. No.

I curled up under my desk. I stayed there for... I don't know how long.

When I crawled out the office was... chairs overturned, a discarded shoe, coats and bags just left.

It was quite nice, quiet like that. I had a wander about. Tried the shoe on but it was too small. I got the key for the stationery cupboard...

She pulls some stationery from her pockets, plus a stapler.

It's Kelvin's. He's always a right prick about it, never lets anyone use it.

Do you need anything stapled?

KATHY. Not right now, thanks.

I suppose you don't know how you'll react until it happens.

Me, after the announcement, I made a cup of tea. Drank it. Then I threw every plate, mug, bowl I had at the wall while screaming bloody murder. Then I made another cup of tea – in my travel mug this time cos I'd smashed all my mugs – drank it, then came down here and put the sign outside for the quiz.

FRAN. Where's Rav got to?

KATHY. He's gone out for a smoke.

FRAN. I should – [follow him]

KATHY. Maybe give him a minute.

FRAN. Oh. Okay.

KATHY. We're a magnet tonight. All the reunions. My brother turned up before –

FRAN. I wouldn't mind a cigarette, too.

KATHY (*stopping her, a hand on her arm?*). Seriously, hold fire.

Have you come far?

FRAN. About forty-five minutes.

KATHY. Walked?

FRAN. Cycled. Someone left their bike in reception.

I haven't ridden in years.

KATHY. You never forget.

FRAN. You do.

Wobbling along, drivers screeching past, rules of the road completely forgotten.

Longest forty-five minutes of my life.

KATHY. What made you point your bike in our direction?

FRAN. I think that's between me and Rav, don't you?

KATHY. Course.

Beat.

FRAN. Has he ever mentioned me?

KATHY. Erm… not that I can think of.

FRAN. He was always quite quiet about his feelings.

KATHY. Was he?

FRAN. I thought he'd remember me, though. Seeing me.

KATHY. He does remember you.

Francesca Burt.

FRAN. Burr.

KATHY. Burr. That's what I said.

It just took him a minute.

FRAN. A bit longer than that.

KATHY. You did land on him out of the blue.

FRAN. I suppose. And I have changed my hair. Lost a bit of weight.

KATHY. There you go, then. Unrecognisable.

And now you've both got your breath back, stopped being sick –

FRAN. I wasn't sick.

KATHY. No, but you can calmly have a chat, say what you cycled here to say, take it from there.

Yeah?

FRAN. Yeah. Okay. Yeah, you're right.

Enter RAV.

RAV. Sorry about that, everyone.

KATHY. Rav –

RAV. Round Three.

KATHY. Do you want me to do that, you two go and have a catch-up?

RAV. No. The end-of-the-world quiz waits for no man, literally.

Onwards ever onwards to our fiery decline.

Round Three.

KATHY. Come and join my team, Fran. I need all the help I can get.

Let him do this round, then you can grab a few minutes.

He's very serious about his quiz-mastering is our Rav.

FRAN. Thanks.

FRAN *sits with* KATHY.

RAV. Round Three – here's your musical clue.

CD player – Lisa Stansfield's 'All Around the World' plays.

Over the intro, RAV *is trying to encourage* KATHY *to get the clue –*

Are you listening, Kathy?

Do you get it? Do you? Do you get it? Kathy?

KATHY. If you'd let me hear it.

She listens, nonplussed.

RAV *joins in with the chorus of the song.*

RAV. Geddit? Around the world? The world?

KATHY. Geography?

RAV. No.

What does the world have?

KATHY. History?

RAV. History?

KATHY. World history.

RAV. Countries. The world has countries. And what do countries have?

KATHY. People?

RAV. Jesus, it's like pulling teeth.

Anyone, what do countries have?

Flags! They have flags. Flags of the world.

KATHY. Yeessss.

RAV. That's right, this one's for you, Kathy. Our very own Peggy Mitchell, our Sid Perks, our… who runs The Rovers these days? I haven't watched *Corrie* since Hayley died. Anyone know?

Hopefully an audience member can supply the answer which, at the time of writing, is Johnny and Jenny Connor.

Our very own Jenny Connor.

Let's hear it for Kathy, everyone. Stand up and take a bow.

RAV *leads the crowd in a round of applause.*

This makes KATHY *emotional again. she wipes away tears.*

KATHY. Sorry. Silly. I keep crying. I'm going to dehydrate if this keeps on.

RAV. Okay, enough of the soppy stuff. Back to the important business of the night.

I'm going to hold up six flags – one at a time – and you have to write down the country they're for.

All clear? Everybody ready?

Kathy, are you ready?

KATHY. I was born ready.

RAV. Round Three. Flags. (*Holding it up.*) FLAG ONE.

KATHY. At least give me a challenge.

RAV. Oooh, she's cocky, ladies and gents. Pride comes before a fall?

FLAG TWO.

KATHY. Please. Piece of piss.

RAV. FLAG THREE.

FRAN (*to* KATHY). That one's –

KATHY. You are not required here, love. Just sit there and look pretty.

RAV. FLAG FOUR.

KATHY. Is this for babies?

RAV. FLAG FIVE.

KATHY. Boom.

RAV. FLAG SIX.

KATHY....

RAV. Oooh, have I stumped her?

Is she stumped? She looks stumped to me.

KATHY. It's between two...

RAV. Anyone need to see any of them again?

Right then, so while Kathy regrets being so insufferably overconfident, if you're all done then everyone swap – you know the drill by now.

While that's happening –

FRAN. Rav, can I talk to you?

RAV. Everybody swapped?

FRAN. I really have to tell you something.

RAV. In a sec.

Okay. All done? Excellent.

Now I'm going to invite Kathy up here to take us through the answers without using the answer sheet. Put her money where her mouth is.

Kathy, if you can join me here please.

No pressure and in your own time, but quickly cos we'll all be dead soon.

Flag One.

KATHY. Wales.

RAV. Flag Two.

KATHY. Switzerland.

RAV. Flag Three.

KATHY. Bosnia and Herzegovina.

FRAN. Sorry, but I really do need to talk to you.

RAV. Flag Four.

KATHY. China.

RAV. Flag Five. She's on a roll.

KATHY. Bahamas.

RAV. And finally, she's got them all right so far but could this one be her undoing?

Drumroll please…

Encourage audience to get drumroll going.

Flag Six. Kathy?

RAV *cuts the drumroll.*

KATHY *takes a big breath in to reveal the answer but* FRAN *beats her to the punch with –*

FRAN. I love you, Rav.

RAV. What?

FRAN. I love you.

RAV. Course you do, I'm very lovable.

Kathy –

FRAN. No. I mean, I *love* you.

Actual heart-pounding, heart-aching, love-of-my-life, romantic love, heart beating out of my chest when I think about you, love you.

RAV. You don't know me.

FRAN. I do.

RAV. We haven't seen each other for years.

FRAN. So?

RAV. So you can't love someone you haven't seen for a decade.

FRAN. Yes I can. I can love whoever I like.

RAV. Well yes, but.

How did you even know where to find me?

FRAN. I follow you on Twitter. And Instagram.

You're not on Facebook, are you?

RAV. No one's on Facebook any more.

KATHY. I am.

FRAN. And you're always posting about this place.

About your day.

About Kathy.

KATHY. What do you say about me?

FRAN. Nothing bad. The funny things you say.

KATHY. Funny ha-ha or funny weird?

FRAN. Both.

I feel like I know you, he talks about you so much.

KATHY (*to* RAV). Do you?

FRAN (*to* RAV). And you. You say I don't know you, but I know you do park runs once a fortnight.

I know you make a really good steak and kidney pie.

I know you love funny cat videos.

RAV. Everyone loves funny cat videos.

FRAN. I know you really hate Paul Hollywood.

RAV. Everyone really hates Paul Hollywood.

FRAN. I know that when you were fourteen you got your best mate Jonesy who was in my Business Studies class to put a note in my rucksack asking if I'd go out with you and I said yes and we went to Fat Mike's All You Can Eat Buffet for our first date and I was so nervous I hardly ate anything which kind of defeated the object of Fat Mike's All You Can Eat Buffet but I didn't want you to think I was greedy and you had corn on the cob and it got all stuck between your teeth and all night all I could think of was that sweetcorn and how if you kissed me it was going to go in my mouth and I really wanted you to kiss me but I didn't want all your sweetcorn in my mouth.

RAV. Okay, and breathe.

FRAN. That year we went out was honestly the happiest year of my life.

RAV. We were kids.

FRAN. So? We still knew how we felt.

Fifteen is a formative age.

And if my parents hadn't split up and Mam got a job down the country.

We tried so hard to get me to stay.

He asked his parents if I could move in with them. But they said we were too young. He was so upset. Weren't you?

RAV. Yeah.

FRAN. Did they stop you replying to my emails too? My calls, my texts.

RAV. They said we were too young, like you said.

FRAN. What I felt for you I've never felt for anyone else.

RAV. You don't mean that.

FRAN. I do. Nothing's come close.

Standing here with you now, it doesn't matter how long it's been. I feel the same fizzy butterflies in my stomach when you look at me. I feel awake.

RAV. Fran –

FRAN. Maybe I shouldn't say this but I'm glad there's an asteroid, cos it's the kick I needed. Seeing that announcement earlier, my life flashed before my eyes and it was… shit.

And after, in the office on my own, your face just kept popping into my mind until you were all I could think about.

I've wasted so much time but I'm here now. And I'm asking you – last chance saloon.

And I know I talk a lot but –

RAV. You always did.

FRAN. Yeah. 'She never says one word when she can say ten' my gran used to say.

Well, here's three – I love you.

I really do.

Sorry, that was six.

And that was another four.

I just wanted to leave it at 'I love you' but I've spoiled it now.

Are you going to say something?

Sorry, that was another six.

RAV *kisses her. It shuts her up.*

KATHY. Ecuador.

The last flag is Ecuador.

BOBBY *enters*.

BOBBY. That car is disgusting.

KATHY. Oh bloody hell.

BOBBY. It should be quarantined.

KATHY. I told you.

BOBBY. Who wants to drive around in a rubbish tip?

KATHY. Yeah, okay, you've made your point.

Have you just come back to complain about the state of my car, or…?

BOBBY. It's a health hazard.

KATHY. Fine. Whatever.

Are we going to get on with this quiz or what?

(*To* RAV.) Oi. Can you detach yourself from her for long enough to read out the next questions or do you want me to do it?

RAV. I can do it.

KATHY. Great.

KATHY *resumes her seat – pencil poised and ready.*

RAV. One sec, everyone. Let me just get my papers in order.

Bobby, welcome back.

Did we say the last flag was Ecuador?

KATHY. Yes.

RAV. Great. Well done. Full house.

Do you want to do a victory lap?

KATHY. No.

RAV. Okay.

Has everyone swapped back?

KATHY. You haven't told us to.

RAV. It's not brain surgery.

Add up the scores from the Flags Round, Round Three, and then swap back.

(*To* KATHY.) What's up with you?

KATHY. Nothing.

RAV. But obviously something.

KATHY. I just... I don't know what's going on. Him here. You and her. Everything's...

Just do the next round, yeah. Everyone's waiting.

FRAN (*to* KATHY). Am I still on your team?

KATHY. If you want.

FRAN *joins* KATHY *who is exuding as much warmth as an ice-cube.*

BOBBY *remains awkwardly standing, nowhere to put himself.*

FRAN (*to* BOBBY). Would you like to be on our team?

KATHY. No sorry, it's full.

I'm sure someone will have you.

(*Picking a team.*) Them. You'll have him, won't you, Bren? I saw you giving him the eye when he walked in before.

BOBBY. I didn't come back to do the quiz.

KATHY. Then what have you come back for? Because I was very clear earlier that I'm not leaving here.

BOBBY. Neither am I now, your car's in a ditch.

KATHY. You drove my car into a ditch?

BOBBY. I got shunted in there by some clown.

KATHY. I've never had one dent in that car, then you take it for five minutes.

BOBBY. They're driving like maniacs out there.

FRAN. He's right, they are.

BOBBY. I might have whiplash, not that you've asked.

RAV. If you're staying, please join a team and sit down.

We're all waiting for you, Bobby. Come on.

It's a brave man who holds up The Horsemen pub quiz.

BOBBY. Fine.

BOBBY *joins a team*.

RAV. Everyone settled? Okay, Round Four. Film and Television.

RAV *starts trying to find the track on the stereo*.

KATHY. Just leave that. No one cares about the music.

FRAN. I care.

A-Ha's 'The Sun Always Shines On TV' plays.

It's barely got going when KATHY *cuts in* –

KATHY. 'The Sun Always Shines on TV'. Yes, very clever. We get it.

RAV *stops the track*.

RAV. This is a side of you I've not seen before, Kathy. I don't like it.

KATHY. I guess we're both showing surprising sides of ourselves tonight.

RAV. Meaning?

KATHY. Round Four. Film and Television.

RAV. Fine.

Everyone ready?

KATHY. Yes, stop faffing about.

RAV. QUESTION ONE. Which member of Monty Python sang the theme tune for the TV series *One Foot in the Grave*?

QUESTION TWO. What was the first name of the character played by Kylie Minogue in *Neighbours*?

QUESTION THREE. James Corden and Ruth Jones wrote which BBC comedy series that returned this Christmas for a special episode?

QUESTION FOUR. Who played Dracula in the 1931 film of the same name?

QUESTION FIVE. Who voiced the forgetful blue tang fish in *Finding Nemo* and *Finding Dory*?

QUESTION SIX. Last question in this round. Who directed the film *Alien*?

KATHY. Is that it? Right. Swap.

(*Snappy at* FRAN.) Swap with them. Them.

FRAN. Sorry.

KATHY. Hurry up, we'll all be dead soon.

RAV. Kathy.

KATHY. What? It's your catchphrase.

RAV. Don't snap at her.

KATHY (*snapping at* FRAN). Did I snap at you?

RAV. Stop it.

KATHY. Ah, the big protector standing up for his woman.

His woman of less than five minutes.

RAV. It's none of your business.

KATHY. When you're snogging up a storm in the middle of my pub, it's my business.

RAV. Jealousy doesn't suit you.

KATHY. What am I jealous of?

RAV. I know you're, you know –

KATHY. What?

RAV. Lonely.

Paul dumped you, we all lived that saga.

KATHY. I dumped Paul, actually. I don't care what he told everyone.

And no, I'm not lonely.

RAV. What's the problem, then?

KATHY. Nothing. Absolutely nothing at all.

You know what, good luck to you.

What's the worst that can happen in an hour? I'm sure it'll be a beautiful and fulfilling relationship from first to last.

FRAN. This is all I've ever wanted, Kathy.

KATHY. And you've got it, well done you.

FRAN. I don't know why you're being horrible.

RAV. Leave her, if she wants to have a cob on that's her problem.

Okay then everyone. Answers to Round Four –

KATHY. I just think…

Forget it.

She's not saying any more.

RAV. Fine.

ANSWER 1. The Monty Python who sang the theme tune was *Eric Idle*.

FRAN. Can I read them out?

RAV. Of course.

FRAN *joins him at the front.*

FRAN. ANSWER TWO. Charlene.

ANSWER THREE. *Gavin and Stacey.*

RAV. Slow down. You need to give them a chance to mark it, and to correct it if it's wrong.

FRAN. Sorry.

RAV. I hope you're all remembering to add the correct answers if they're wrong.

FRAN. ANSWER FOUR. Bela Lugosi.

ANSWER FIVE. Ellen DeGeneres.

ANSWER SIX: *Ridley Scott* directed *Alien*.

I love that film.

RAV. Me too.

BOTH. 'Get away from her, you bitch'.

FRAN *kisses* RAV *again*.

KATHY. Oh, for God's sake.

RAV. Spit it out, woman, before it chokes you.

KATHY. You're gay.

RAV. What are you basing that on?

KATHY. I don't know. You.

How you are.

RAV. How I am?

KATHY. That jacket, your manner.

RAV. My jacket and my manner?

So, tired stereotype and lazy assumption?

KATHY. No.

Well, maybe yes but no.

RAV. I am so disappointed in you, Kathy.

And this is your jacket, actually.

KATHY. I know.

RAV. And I'm sorry if I look better in it than you.

KATHY. See. That's the kind of thing a gay person would say.

RAV. 'The kind of thing a gay person would say'? Can you hear yourself?

KATHY. I don't mean it like, offensive.

I'm sorry.

So you're not gay?

RAV. Oh, I am gay but I've never told you that. And I certainly didn't tell this room full of people.

KATHY. I just assumed you didn't think you had to.

I don't mind. I'm sure no one minds.

RAV. Oh well, as long as no one minds.

KATHY. No, I don't mean… I just mean… Oh God.

RAV. I think you should just stop talking.

KATHY. Yeah.

RAV. Yeah.

FRAN. Yeah.

They all blink at FRAN *– forgot she was there.*

I, erm… I'll be back in a minute.

RAV. Fran –

But she's gone.

Happy now?

KATHY. I'm sorry.

Exit RAV *after* FRAN.

Shit.

BOBBY *sidles over to* KATHY *from his table.*

Shut up.

BOBBY. I didn't say anything.

Silence.

You've done the place out.

KATHY. What?

BOBBY. I noticed as soon as I walked in…

KATHY. You'd have known if you'd ever been in.

Should I go after him?

BOBBY. I wouldn't for now.

KATHY. Shit.

But seeing them together, I mean…

BOBBY. Jealous?

KATHY. No. Why does everyone think I'm jealous?

A single woman over forty, she must be desperate for a man and bitter towards anyone who's got one.

BOBBY. What then?

KATHY. He's gay.

And I know I'm not the only one who just assumed…

Yeah, you can all look away but I know.

Bill, you were always saying what a catch he'd be for your Michael.

How is it fair on him? Or her? Surely you can't just *not* be gay?

BOBBY. Isn't that for him to decide?

KATHY. Urgh, what a mess.

Beat.

So do you like it?

BOBBY. What?

KATHY. What I've done with the place?

BOBBY. It still smells of stale beer and piss.

KATHY. Right.

Actually, you know what, everyone, why don't you stretch your legs, go to the loo, grab another drink if your glass is empty.

We'll come back in ten for the last round.

I think Rav's got something special up his sleeve, so that'll be… yeah.

KATHY *turns the CD back on – Cher's 'If I Could Turn Back Time' plays.*

BOBBY. Kathy –

KATHY. I just need five minutes, Bobby. Okay.

You know your way around, it hasn't changed that much.

KATHY *exits.*

The music continues on the stereo – various tracks throughout the interval.

End of Act One.

ACT TWO

KATHY *reappears. She's touched up her lipstick and is back in composed, in-charge, landlady mode.*

She turns the stereo off.

KATHY. Right, everyone, welcome back.

I hope you had a good break? I know I did. Sometimes you just need a big wee and things don't seem so bad.

Is Bobby...? Has Bobby gone?

Looking, he's not there.

Right.

Right. I don't know why I'd expect anything different.

Well if it's okay with you, let's check in and see if there's any update on our fiery friend up there –

S*he turns the stereo's radio back on – the same recorded broadcast from the start of the play is still repeating. It's more fragmented, more static, until it jams –*

VOICE....an Emergency Broadcast... not a test... asteroid... collision course... impact imminent... NASA... failed... a World-Ending Event... Recommended action... thoughts and prayers...

...thoughts and prayers...

...thoughts and prayers...

...thoughts and prayers...

KATHY *turns it off.*

KATHY. Okay. Good. Well, not good, the opposite of good, but... Okay.

Now, unfortunately, it doesn't look like Rav's coming back to finish the quiz and the night's not getting any younger and that asteroid isn't getting any further away.

So, shall we just add up the scores from the rounds we've already done and that be that?

I know it's not what was promised, and I hate to let you down, for that to be the last thing I do on this earth, but...

BOBBY. I'm sure we can think of some questions for the last round.

KATHY. I thought you'd gone.

BOBBY. I was just having a piss. Sometimes a big wee –

KATHY. And things don't seem so bad.

BOBBY. Yeah.

KATHY. How's the whiplash?

BOBBY. If we survive this and there's a claim to be had, it's agony.

But otherwise, it's alright. Bren gave me some painkillers.

KATHY. Did she now?

Right, everyone, count up those scores.

And we need to choose the Best Team Name as well.

BOBBY. Come on, it can't be that hard to think up some questions.

KATHY. Don't let Rav hear you say that.

BOBBY. Got one – what was Joe Strummer's original stage name?

KATHY. No one's going to know that.

BOBBY. They might.

Does anyone know the answer? Joe Strummer's original stage name?

The answer is Woody Mellor.

If the audience say yes and know it, then BOBBY *can be, like, 'see'.*

If no one pipes up or get it wrong, KATHY *can be, like, 'see'.*

BOBBY. Okay, right, here's another one –

KATHY. Not about The Clash.

BOBBY. Oh.

KATHY. Or if it is, then easy: The Clash.

BOBBY. The Clash's most famous album is called *where_* Calling?

KATHY. Okay, yeah. That's Question One to Round – what Round is this?

Round Five.

Wait, we should do it properly.

Round Five – Miscellaneous.

Pick a song. The CD cover is there –

BOBBY *reads CD sleeve carefully.*

In your own time.

BOBBY. It's a bit of a weird mix.

KATHY. Just pick one. The vibe is dying.

BOBBY. What vibe?

KATHY. Okay well, we're dying in – what? – half an hour? So pick one.

BOBBY. Got it.

The Clash's 'Four Horsemen' starts to play.

KATHY. What's that?

BOBBY. What's that? The Clash.

KATHY. Actually yeah, it does sound familiar. I remember it thudding through your wall into my bedroom.

Okay. Round Five, Question One.

She goes to turn the track off but he stops her –

BOBBY. Hang on. (*Sings and/or dances along a few lines.*)

KATHY. Very good. Finished?

She turns the track off.

Question One. The Clash's most famous album is called *where* Calling?

I've still got all your Clash posters, you know. Your albums.

Dad wanted to chuck it all after you went, but I rescued them. I put them in the loft.

BOBBY. He wanted to chuck it all? He loved them more than I did.

KATHY. You broke his heart, Bobby.

BOBBY. Question Two. What is a group of owls called?

KATHY. Where did you pull that from?

BOBBY. Mo at work has an owl calendar on her desk, each month has different facts. That was this month's.

KATHY. The working days must just fly by.

BOBBY. Question Three.

KATHY. I've got a question.

BOBBY. Okay.

KATHY. Why did you come here tonight?

BOBBY. Kathy.

KATHY. I don't think it's unreasonable to want to know.

BOBBY. We're getting on, don't spoil it.

KATHY. I'm not. I just want to know why after twenty years refusing to darken the doors.

BOBBY. To get you.

KATHY. You knew I wouldn't leave. We've established that.

BOBBY. To see you, then.

KATHY. Why?

BOBBY. You're my sister, do I need a reason?

KATHY. It hasn't been enough of a reason before.

BOBBY. We weren't about to get wiped out before.

KATHY. Dad being wiped out wasn't a reason. Or Mum.

BOBBY. I came to their funerals.

KATHY. You did, yeah.

Sat at the back, didn't say hello or goodbye.

BOBBY. I didn't think you'd want to see me.

KATHY. Why would I not want to see you?

BOBBY. Alright, I didn't want to see you.

KATHY. Why not?

I never did anything to you, Bobby.

BOBBY. You…

KATHY. Yeah? Go on, I'd love to know.

BOBBY. Question Three. What is…

KATHY. Question Three. What did I do to you?

BOBBY. Question Three. What is the biggest…

KATHY. Question Three. What did I do to you, Bobby?

BOBBY. Stop it. Everyone's looking.

KATHY. Good.

Come on, tell me. Tell me. Tell me.

BOBBY. Stop it.

KATHY. It.

BOBBY. You're being ridiculous.

KATHY. Ridiculous.

BOBBY. Let's just do this.

KATHY. This.

BOBBY. Get it done.

KATHY. Done.

BOBBY. Then we can be annihilated and it's finished.

KATHY. Finished.

BOBBY. That is so annoying.

KATHY. Annoying.

BOBBY. Stop it.

KATHY. It.

BOBBY. I mean it.

KATHY. It.

BOBBY (*blurts out, frustrated*). I see things, okay.

KATHY. What things?

BOBBY. On Facebook.

KATHY. What things?

BOBBY. You know, the pub's Facebook page.

KATHY. You follow us?

BOBBY. Yeah.

> In the photos you're always laughing and smiling. The pub looks fresh and light, it's packed. Everything's rosy.

KATHY. Okay.

BOBBY. I wanted to see it for myself.

> Cos laughing-and-smiling photos, they're the lies that Facebook is built on, aren't they?

KATHY. We're hardly going to post pictures of the place when it's dead, of me with bags under my eyes from worrying about paying the suppliers next month.

BOBBY. Are you in trouble?

KATHY. No. But only cos of my hard work. No one helped me, no one taught me.

BOBBY. It's what you wanted, though.

KATHY. Yeah, but some support would have been nice.

Dad would have held your hand through it all. Me, he practically threw the keys at me and never said another word.

BOBBY. That's not my fault.

KATHY. I'm not saying it is.

You're allowed to not want this place – but to turn your back on us all so completely. To turn your back on me.

BOBBY. It wasn't like that.

KATHY. It feels like that.

BOBBY. You and this place, you're the same thing.

KATHY. No we're not.

BOBBY. You're spending your final hours here hosting a pub quiz.

KATHY. Okay, well, yes. Maybe we are the same thing.

Maybe that's the biggest compliment you could give me, actually.

Rav, before, he called me queen of this kingdom and it made me feel so…

This place, Bobby. It's like being a ringmaster of all human experience.

It's amazing. It's an honour.

Had a baby – go for a drink.

Got a promotion – go for a drink.

Lost your job – go for a drink.

Had a good day, had a bad day.

Your team lost, your team won.

You got dumped, you dumped somebody.

Your friends are here, your friends aren't here.

It's cold – there's a fire. It's hot – there's a beer garden.

You just don't want to be on your own – go for a drink.

Remember what Dad used to say?

BOBBY. Dad said a lot of things.

KATHY. That 'pub' to humans is the equivalent of 'walkies' to dogs.

BOBBY. Yeah.

KATHY. And I know you think this is stupid here tonight, but it's actually never been more important. We've never been more needed.

Even if it's to forget, to bury our heads in the sand.

The real world can't get us in here.

BOBBY. It can. A flaming lump of rock and metal hurtling down from space will get us anywhere –

KATHY. Yeah, but you know what I mean.

BOBBY. I can't see it the way you can.

All I remember is Dad having a laugh and a comment for every punter who walked in here, but he couldn't string a sentence together over the family dinner table.

KATHY. I get that.

I remember that.

BOBBY. He gave all of himself to this place and never had time for us.

KATHY. He worshipped you.

BOBBY. Only for as long as he thought I was learning at his knee. When I showed even a hint of wanting something else…

KATHY. He was hard on both of us.

BOBBY. You were his princess.

KATHY. I wasn't though, was I? And he didn't like that.

BOBBY. I just... I had to know.

KATHY. Know what?

BOBBY. If it was right, what I was seeing. The smiling faces, the fresh paint.

KATHY. And is it?

BOBBY. Yeah.

KATHY. And you're proud, yeah? That I've done it. That I've made it work.

FRAN *storms in, interrupting.* RAV *follows.*

RAV. If you'd just let me explain –

FRAN *retrieves her coat/bag. She's leaving.*

KATHY. What's going on?

FRAN. Ask him.

KATHY. What's going on?

FRAN. It's all his fault.

KATHY. What is?

FRAN. My whole life.

KATHY. Okay.

FRAN. My whole stupid shitty sodding stupid life.

RAV. It's not stupid or shitty.

FRAN. I'm not talking to you. Poof.

KATHY. Whoa, now. We don't have that kind of language in here, lady.

BOBBY. Do you want me to throw her out?

KATHY. I can throw her out if she needs throwing out.

(*To* RAV.) Do you want her throwing out?

RAV. No.

FRAN. I'm sorry.

KATHY. It's not me you should be apologising to, it's him.

FRAN. No chance.

He should be apologising to me for wasting my time.

RAV. We were teenagers.

FRAN. Not just now we weren't.

(*To* KATHY.) What is it you said? – 'snogging up a storm'.

RAV. Isn't that what you came for?

FRAN. No. Yes but, not *just* that. So much more than that.

And you made me think that... (*She's leaving.*)

RAV. You can't go.

FRAN. You've made it clear you don't want me to stay.

RAV. I didn't say that.

FRAN. But what you say isn't worth squat, is it? You're a liar.

(*To* KATHY.) I'd watch yourself with him. It's pathological. He's probably had his hands in the till as well.

RAV. I wouldn't do that.

KATHY. I know you wouldn't.

(*To* FRAN.) These are some big claims you're making.

FRAN. Are you going to tell her or shall I?

Fine.

He never asked his parents if I could stay. When my mam was moving us away after GCSEs. He said he asked them and they said no, but he's just let slip that he never even asked them.

KATHY. Is that right?

FRAN. You told me to my face that you asked them, you promised me.

RAV. I know I did.

FRAN. You called your mam a 'bitch' for not letting me. You never spoke badly about her.

RAV. I shouldn't have done that.

But she'd have said no, anyway. There was no chance.

FRAN. That's not the point.

All these years you've let me think it was them who kept us apart.

Did they stop you answering my texts too?

Be honest.

RAV. No.

FRAN. So you just ignored me? Out of sight out of mind?

RAV. We were so young. We were too young, Fran.

I liked you, I did, but not like that –

FRAN. Cos you're gay? Did you know that then, laughing at me?

RAV. No.

FRAN. Cos you asked me out, don't forget.

RAV. I know. But once we started. All I knew is that I didn't like you the same as you liked me.

And when you moved away – I was relieved. I'm sorry, but I was.

I never thought for a minute you'd still be so… hung up on me.

FRAN. I'm not 'hung up', I'm…

After we moved away, I didn't know a soul. I know no one does when they go somewhere new, but I couldn't find where I fit.

Mam said I needed to stop pining and get on with it. And I did.

I've got friends. A career. Well, a job.

I've had other boyfriends. I've got a boyfriend now. Well, I did have. I don't know if we're still – . Probably not. Steve.

KATHY. And what does Steve think about all this?

FRAN. Dunno. Last time I saw him he was digging a hole in the garden, said he was going to build a bunker.

BOBBY. Not such a bad idea.

FRAN. It doesn't matter though, cos he – all of them – they're not a patch on you, Rav.

None of them would gently brush the annoying bit of hair out of my eyes, or open doors for me, or walk on the outside next to roads in case a car splashed past.

RAV. Did I? I don't think I did do that.

FRAN. The way I remember it you did.

RAV. I know when we went to Maccie D's I'd let you have my gherkins.

FRAN. And over the years, the more I've thought about it, the surer I am that my life started drifting off track when we split up.

So if we hadn't. If we were together then things would be right.

This isn't how it was meant to go, though. I'd walk in and you'd sweep me into your arms and there'd be music and fireworks and –

Saying it all out loud, am I insane?

KATHY/RAV/BOBBY. Erm...

KATHY. It could be worse.

FRAN. How?

BOBBY. You could have killed a duck.

KATHY/RAV/FRAN. What?

BOBBY (to KATHY). You remember. Jan Blanchard. She had that pet duck she used to carry around everywhere.

KATHY. Oh yeah, what was it called?

BOBBY. You can't have forgotten. Quack the Ripper.

KATHY. Quack the Ripper. God she was weird.

BOBBY. So poor Quack the Ripper. Jan was never without him.

RAV. Where did she get a duck from?

BOBBY. God knows.

Then one day, she went to put it back in its cage and it was dead.

She killed it. She held on too tight, smothered it.

FRAN. What's that got to do with me?

BOBBY. She loved that duck too much. Too hard.

She suffocated it with love. Literally.

No one has an answer to that.

FRAN. Why did you kiss me before? The truth.

RAV. You said that you loved me.

FRAN. Right.

RAV. No one's ever said that to me before.

I wanted to die being loved.

It didn't matter if you were a boy or a girl. Love's love, isn't it.

KATHY. Oh, sweetheart.

RAV. It was nice, to be in someone's heart like that. I liked it.

FRAN. You don't feel the same about me, though?

RAV. No.

But I can pretend for however long we've got left.

Hold doors open for you, brush your hair out of your eyes.

FRAN. But it wouldn't be real?

RAV. Does it matter?

FRAN. It does, yeah.

RAV. Then no. I'm sorry.

FRAN. Oh Christ, what have I done?

I've wasted all this time hankering after some fantasy.

RAV. I'm sorry.

FRAN. Oh God.

Can I have a drink, please? A double. A triple.

KATHY. Coming up.

KATHY *goes to get* FRAN *a drink.*

FRAN *is starting to panic.*

FRAN. Oh my God.

I can't breathe.

RAV. It's okay, you're alright.

BOBBY. Get a paper bag.

Has anyone got a paper bag?

RAV. Put your head between your knees.

BOBBY. That's when you're going to faint.

RAV. Is it?

KATHY *returns – she's got* FRAN*'s drink and some packets of crisps.*

KATHY. What's happening?

Is she okay?

BOBBY *tips out one of the packets of crisps and gives it to* FRAN *to breathe into –*

BOBBY. Try and slow your breathing down.

Breathe in and out of the bag.

In and out. Slowly.

Slowly.

Etc, etc.

FRAN *does. Gradually her breathing regulates.*

There.

You're alright. You're okay.

RAV. Okay?

FRAN. Yeah.

Yeah.

KATHY. Well done. Where did you learn that?

BOBBY. Mo led a first-aid course at work.

FRAN. I'm sorry. I'm so sorry, all of you.

KATHY. It's fine.

FRAN. It's really not. Rav –

RAV. Forget it.

FRAN. Yeah, but –

RAV. Forget it.

Crisp? They're not gherkins, but cheese and onion is close.

FRAN. I think I've gone mad.

KATHY. Not at all. A good night's sleep, things will look better tomorrow.

FRAN. There is no tomorrow.

KATHY. Oh. Yeah. Sorry.

FRAN. This is really happening, isn't it?

An asteroid really is going to hit us and we're really all going to die.

KATHY. Don't upset yourself again.

Drink your drink.

FRAN. It's like something out of a film.

Bruce Willis should be up there blowing it up, or something.

BOBBY. They tried that. It barely made a dint.

FRAN. Yeah well, if they'd sent a proper astronaut instead of Bruce Willis, they'd have had more luck.

BOBBY. No. I didn't mean –

FRAN. I know. I'm joking. It was a joke.

BOBBY. Right. Funny.

FRAN. Aren't any of you scared? You don't seem scared.

KATHY. Oh I'm scared, love.

RAV. Terrified.

BOBBY. Shitting it.

Silence.

RAV. Round Five?

BOBBY. Yeah.

FRAN. Yes.

KATHY. Great.

BOBBY. We made a start –

RAV. What?

BOBBY. Kathy and I – we made up a couple of questions but we got a bit sidetracked.

RAV. Right, no, absolutely not.

BOBBY. You abandoned post.

RAV. There's been stuff going on, in case you hadn't noticed.

I'm back now, though.

BOBBY. We were just trying to help.

RAV. Scribble out whatever drivel they asked you, we're starting Round Five again.

I can't believe you thought you could just jump in. What a liberty.

KATHY. Sorry.

BOBBY. It's just a stupid quiz.

RAV. Excuse me? Sorry? What?

KATHY. Bobby.

BOBBY. What? It is.

RAV. This quiz is curated, not just any old questions you can pull out your arse.

BOBBY (*mocking*). 'Curated.'

RAV. Yes. It means crafted.

BOBBY. I know what curated means.

RAV. Okay then. Everyone ready? Round Five –

BOBBY. Hell of a way to spend your last night on earth.

KATHY. I thought we'd just been through this?

BOBBY. Yeah, not him though.

I get why you're here. Sort of.

But him.

RAV. Erm, you're here too.

BOBBY. Yeah with my sister.

(*Re: the audience.*) And all this lot are here with their friends, family, neighbours.

(*Re:* FRAN.) Even she came to be with the love of her life, however misguided. Poor cow.

FRAN. Oi.

RAV. Don't talk about her like that.

BOBBY. What, cos you've been so respectful to her tonight?

I mean, to be fair, if I was in your shoes.

RAV. What shoes are they?

BOBBY. Here. On your own.

RAV. I'm not on my own.

BOBBY. Who's here for you?

RAV. Look around you.

BOBBY. Customers.

RAV. And Kathy.

BOBBY. Your boss.

KATHY. I'm more than his boss. We're friends.

BOBBY. Work friends.

It's like me sitting in the office with Mo tonight.

KATHY. You talk about her enough. Maybe you'd like to be.

BOBBY. Haven't you got anywhere else you could be? What about any family?

RAV. What about them?

BOBBY. Did you try to get to them?

RAV. No.

BOBBY. What, they don't approve or...?

RAV. Don't approve of what?

BOBBY. You know.

RAV. I don't know.

BOBBY. Of your... I mean... your lifestyle.

KATHY. For God's sake, Bobby.

BOBBY. I don't know, do I?

RAV. My family love me and I love them. I don't need to come huffing over hill and dale for seven hours to make peace –

BOBBY. Who said I came to make peace?

RAV. There's nowhere else I want to be right now than here.

BOBBY. Fine.

I mean it's a bit pathetic, but. Cool. Knock yourself out with your little quiz. Round Five.

RAV. At least I'm wanted here.

BOBBY. Sorry?

RAV. All these friends, family, neighbours – I know them. They know me. A smile, a jibe, a nod.

And maybe I just pull them pints, but that's more than you do.

BOBBY. You don't know anything about me.

RAV. And you me.

BOBBY. I was born in this pub.

KATHY. No you weren't. You were born in St Mary's, same as me.

BOBBY. You know what I mean.

I grew up here. This is my home.

KATHY. That you rejected.

BOBBY. Yes but you know what I mean.

RAV. I know what you mean.

And I know that most people in here couldn't pick you out of a line-up.

I certainly didn't know you existed until an hour ago.

BOBBY. So? Family's family.

RAV. Is it?

It takes more than blood to be family.

BOBBY. It literally doesn't.

KATHY. Yes it does.

It absolutely does.

We might not be blood but Roz there, she comes round once a month and we drink gin and watch true-crime documentaries.

Shelley, she does hot yoga with me once a week even though she's not very bendy and she hates being hot.

And Tommo and Max, they took turns taking me to my hospital appointments so I didn't have to sit by myself.

BOBBY. What hospital appointments?

KATHY. And Rav here –

BOBBY. What hospital appointments?

KATHY. It doesn't matter.

BOBBY. Well, now I feel shit.

RAV. Good.

KATHY. Yeah. Good.

BOBBY. You could have come to me.

KATHY. I didn't know where you were.

I asked Mum for your number but she said you didn't want it given out.

I wrote letters for her to pass on, never heard back.

I only know you got married – that I'm an auntie – cos I'd see the Christmas cards on her mantel. 'Love Bobby'. 'Love Bobby and Fiona'. 'Love Bobby, Fiona and the girls'.

BOBBY. I had to have a clean break.

KATHY. There was nothing 'clean' about it. It was messy and it was cruel.

Silence. They blink at each other.

KATHY *breaks away first.*

Come on, Rav, Round Five.

RAV. Are you okay?

KATHY. I'm fine. I'm great.

RAV. Yeah, you are great. And never forget that.

A pointed look at BOBBY *who can't hold* RAV*'s gaze.*

Elsewhere, FRAN *is leaving.*

KATHY. Where are you going, love?

FRAN. I don't know.

KATHY. You haven't got time to get anywhere.

FRAN. No?

KATHY. 'Fraid not.

Sit with me, yeah. Finish the quiz.

FRAN. I've made such a fool of myself.

KATHY. No. You didn't want to have any regrets, that's not foolish.

FRAN. Do you have regrets?

KATHY. Course.

RAV. Okay. Round Five. At last.

The final round. And I mean final.

And in honour of the impending catastrophe this last round is all about Space.

CD player – The Firm's 'Star Trekkin'' plays.

RAV *gets his papers together and the like.*

Everybody ready?

Bobby?

BOBBY, *who has been hovering with nowhere to put himself, joins the quiz table he was at previously.*

RAV *turns the track off.*

Okay. The end is nigh. And not just of this quiz.

Pens down. Eyes up. Let's go.

QUESTION ONE. Some planets have millions of tiny rocks circling their equator which look like – *what*?

QUESTION TWO. What was the name of the first satellite that was sent into space?

QUESTION THREE. Ganymede is a moon of which planet?

QUESTION FOUR. Which is the coldest planet in the solar system?

QUESTION FIVE. The first woman in space Valentina Tereshkova is from which country?

QUESTION SIX. Last question in this round and of the whole quiz. Which planet in our solar system is the only one not to be named after a Greek or Roman deity and – extra clue – is about to be hit by a life-ending asteroid?

Anyone need anything repeating?

Okay, and for the last time – swap those answer sheets.

Everybody swaps.

KATHY. Before Rav gives the final –

RAV. And I mean final –

KATHY. And he means final answers, can we have a moment of appreciation for him, please. He pulled all this together at short notice and I think you'll agree he's done an excellent job.

KATHY *leads a round of applause.*

RAV. Stop, please please. I'm embarrassed.

No I'm not, keep going.

But, no, let's not get ahead of yourselves, it's not finished yet.

KATHY. I thought that was the final (and you mean final) round?

RAV. I've still got some tricks up my sleeve.

KATHY. Intriguing.

RAV. We'll get there.

Okay. Remember, one point per correct answer. If they get it wrong, a big smug cross and write the correct answer alongside it.

ANSWER ONE. The millions of tiny rocks look like *rings*.

ANSWER TWO. Sputnik.

ANSWER THREE. Ganymede is a moon of *Jupiter*.

ANSWER FOUR. *Neptune* is the coldest planet as it's the furthest from the sun.

ANSWER FIVE. Valentina Tereshkova is from *Russia*.

Anyone know the year she went into space? No bonus points, just wondering. (*It's 1963.*)

ANSWER SIX. Last answer. And if you got this wrong – shame on you.

Earth is the only planet in our solar system not to be named after a Greek or Roman deity and is about to be hit by a life-ending asteroid.

Great. And now please tot up their scores for that round *and* their total scores for the whole quiz, then write it nice and big on the front page.

My glamorous assistant Kathy will then drift amongst you and collect all of the sheets so we can reveal the winner.

If the sheet you're marking hasn't got a team name on it, please pass it back so they can add one.

That happens to a blast of music from the stereo – R.E.M.'s 'It's the End of the World as We Know it'.

Once KATHY *has collected all of the answer sheets she returns to* RAV *with them.*

Is that all of them?

KATHY. I think so.

Any more for any more?

That's it.

RAV. Great.

I'm going to go off to a quiet corner to see who's won. I'll leave you in the capable hands of Queen Kathy.

RAV *exits with all of the answer sheets.*

KATHY *turns the music off.*

KATHY. Worra night, eh.

Shall I crack out the karaoke machine?

I know you're all dying to hear my Madonna one last time.

And Jacs, you could do Meatloaf, 'I Would Do Anything For Love'. We might not have time for the whole song, but...

Fran, are you much of a karaoke-er?

FRAN. I can be.

KATHY. What's your song?

FRAN. I like a bit of Whitney.

KATHY. Ambitious.

BOBBY. Me and you always used to do Elton and Kiki Dee. Remember?

Those family holidays to Spain, we'd be first up in the bar on a night.

Remember?

KATHY. Yeah.

BOBBY *starts singing Elton John and Kiki Dee's 'Don't Go Breaking My Heart'. He leaves a gap for* KATHY *to echo but she doesn't. He keeps singing but* KATHY*'s not joining in. He trails off.*

BOBBY (*to* FRAN). Elton John was married to a woman once, so you know. There's hope.

FRAN. I'm not ready to laugh about it yet, thanks.

Do you mind if I see what the news is saying?

KATHY. Go ahead.

FRAN *turns the radio on but there's just static.*

They try to tune into anything. eventually they hit on 'Jerusalem' or 'God Save the Queen' – something patriotic and hopeless.

FRAN. That's not good.

KATHY/BOBBY. No.

It drones on for a bit.

KATHY. Turn it off.

FRAN *does.*

FRAN. Shall we, I don't know, say a prayer or something?

KATHY. Are you religious?

FRAN. No, but it seems like the kind of thing we should do.

Just in case, you know. Hedge our bets.

BOBBY. It might be a bit late.

KATHY. I'll pray with you.

FRAN. Join in, anyone who wants to.

They bow their heads. stand in silence for a moment until –

I don't really know what to say.

KATHY. How about – (*Starts singing Madonna's 'Like a Prayer'.*)

BOBBY. For God's sake, Kathy.

KATHY. What? I'm just joking.

FRAN. I'm going to go and see what the sky's doing.

KATHY. Sorry, I was just… I didn't mean to offend you.

But FRAN*'s gone.*

Ooops.

Silence.

KATHY *and* BOBBY *are uncomfortable together.*

Neither knows what to say or is willing to say what should be said.

BOBBY. How long does it take to count up who's won a bloody pub quiz?

KATHY. Give him a chance.

More silence, then they go to speak together –

Bobby –

BOBBY. Kathy –

You go.

KATHY. You.

BOBBY. No, you.

KATHY. You.

BOBBY. I'm sorry for not getting in touch.

KATHY. Okay.

BOBBY. If I'd known it was for something important. Hospital appointments…?

KATHY. I had a scare a year or so ago. Well, a bit more than a scare.

But I'm fine now. All clear.

BOBBY. Good. Good.

What were you going to say?

KATHY. Is that it?

BOBBY. Erm, yeah.

KATHY. Bloody hell, Bobby.

All I've ever wanted is for you to come back and see this place and say you're proud of me.

When you came bursting in tonight I couldn't believe it. For a second I thought this is it – he's come all this way to say it. But you didn't.

Then before, when you were talking about seeing all the photos on our Facebook page.

But still you haven't actually said it.

And I can't let my disappointment about that be my final thoughts on this earth. I won't.

I'm proud of myself and that's enough. It has to be.

BOBBY. What do you regret?

KATHY. Sorry?

BOBBY. Before. Fran asked you if you have regrets and you said yes.

KATHY. Yeah.

BOBBY. Which are?

KATHY. Well, Paul, obviously.

BOBBY. Who's Paul?

KATHY. Over there. Long story.

Other than that, the usual I expect.

That I didn't have more fun. More sex. More puddings.

That I didn't read more. Take more holidays.

Mainly the sex, though.

BOBBY. But not this place? You never regret staying?

KATHY. Never.

BOBBY. But it's so small and stifling. We were meant to get out, be more.

KATHY. That's how you felt, not me.

BOBBY. I know. And I did it. I got out and yet…

If it's not this place that's small then…

If it's not this place holding me back, then…

KATHY. You've done well for yourself.

BOBBY. How do you know?

KATHY. I don't, but. You must have a job – you and your desk-buddy Mo?

BOBBY. Yes.

KATHY. Do you have somewhere to live?

BOBBY. Yes.

KATHY. Okay, then.

You've got Fiona and the girls. What are their names, by the way?

BOBBY. Amy and Catherine.

KATHY. Catherine?

BOBBY. Yeah.

KATHY. How old?

BOBBY. Fourteen. They're twins.

KATHY. Twins? Bloody hell.

(*Gentle*.) And why… why aren't you with them?

This upsets BOBBY. KATHY *goes to comfort him but he flinches away.*

BOBBY. I'm fine.

I'm fine.

They live in Ireland.

KATHY. Okay.

BOBBY. Have done for – what? – six years now. Fiona remarried and moved back…

KATHY. Right.

BOBBY. I'm middle-management, I live in a house I can barely afford, divorced with two daughters who I barely see and when I do they look at me like… (*Pulls a face.*)

KATHY. They're teenagers, that's just their faces.

BOBBY. It's more than that.

I was meant to *be* something.

KATHY. We all think we're going to be something.

BOBBY. But you are.

KATHY. Am I?

BOBBY. Queen of the kingdom. Ringmaster of this circus.

Happy.

And that's pissed me right off.

I didn't want the happy photos to be right. I came tonight because I wanted the last thing I saw on this earth to be you miserable and defeated so I could know I'd made the right choice.

KATHY. You don't mean that.

BOBBY. I do.

KATHY. That's what you walked seven hours for?

BOBBY. Yeah.

As I got nearer and nearer I was thinking that *can't* be the reason, but it was. It's what propelled me out my front door.

KATHY. To see me miserable and defeated?

BOBBY. Yeah.

KATHY. Bobby, that's…

I'm not going to apologise for not being miserable and defeated.

For getting what I wanted and doing it well.

For not being like you.

BOBBY. A failure?

KATHY. You said it, not me.

They stand apart. Irrevocably broken?

At some point during the above, FRAN *returned and heard most of the exchange.*

FRAN *starts to sing 'Don't Go Breaking My Heart' but it becomes apparent that she doesn't actually know the words.*

KATHY *and* BOBBY *just stare at her.*

She trails off –

FRAN. You said you sang it as kids…?

KATHY/BOBBY.…

FRAN. Sorry, I just thought… a nice memory?

My gran used to say 'don't go to bed on a fight'. Well, don't be wiped off the face of the earth on an argument.

BOBBY. It's not as catchy.

FRAN. No.

Sorry.

KATHY. What's the sky looking like out there, Fran?

FRAN. Ominous.

A decision –

KATHY *starts to sing 'Don't Go Breaking My Heart'.* BOBBY *joins in. They sing together.*

KATHY. You're not a failure.

BOBBY. Okay.

KATHY. You're a twat, but you're not a failure.

BOBBY. Fair enough.

KATHY. I'm glad you came.

BOBBY. Really?

KATHY. Yeah. Even if was for an awful reason.

BOBBY. I'm glad too.

KATHY. Yeah?

BOBBY. Yeah.

They hug tight.

RAV *bounds in.*

RAV. Right then, folks.

FRAN. Shhh, they're having a moment.

KATHY. It's okay, go on.

RAV (*re:* KATHY AND BOBBY). No idea what I've missed but – it's all good, yes?

KATHY. Yeah, it's good.

RAV. Great.

So, the moment of truth has arrived.

Not that moment – (*The asteroid.*) I think we've got a few minutes left, but this very important moment. The scores.

In last place with [lowest score] points out of a possible thirty points is [team name].

Put your hands up.

And so on from last place to first place.

As he goes through them he hands the answer sheets back to the teams (important for later).

But the winners, with an unassailable [highest score] points is [winning team name].

If there's a tie-break, a tie-break question can be asked

TIE-BREAK QUESTION: To the nearest whole number, how many times will England fit into the State of Texas? Nearest answer wins.

The answer is five.

And so we have a winner! Congratulations to [winning team name].

RAV *leads round of applause.*

And we do have a prize.

A certificate appears:

'This is to certify that Team _____ are the winners of The Four Horsemen's End of The World Quiz …' (Or similar.)

And as for the winning Team Name. I've written them all down here and I'm going to let my esteemed friend and colleague Kathy decide.

KATHY. I'm honoured. I will consult, if I may, with my brother dearest.

RAV. Of course.

He gives her a sheet of team names to go through.

While they do that –

Those two seem to have made up.

FRAN. An impending apocalypse will do that.

RAV. Yeah.

Silence. Awkward.

I don't know what to say to you.

FRAN. Same.

RAV. And I'm never lost for words. You take my breath away.

FRAN. Don't take the mick.

RAV. I'm not. I mean it.

You did something so brave –

FRAN. So embarrassing.

RAV. No. You took a chance. I've never done that.

There's this lad in town. He works in the little Tesco on the high street.

I'm in there all the time buying things I don't need, but I've never built up the courage to speak to him.

FRAN. You could go now. You might make it.

RAV. I've got to finish the quiz.

FRAN. It's done, isn't it? Kathy can do Best Team Name.

RAV. Oh, it's not done. Not yet.

Anyway, he might – you know.

FRAN. Reject you? Yeah, that would be humiliating.

RAV. I wish I could give you what you wanted.

FRAN. It's not your fault.

And at least I tried, you know. I did something. Better late than never.

RAV. Better late than pregnant. (*So inappropriate*.)

Sorry.

And Steve's bunker wouldn't have had a quiz, would it?

FRAN. No.

Curated, right?

RAV. That's right.

They share a smile. Some sort of truce/understanding.

KATHY. Okay, we've made our decision.

The Best Team Name –

RAV. For five hundred pounds?

KATHY. For one hundred pounds.

RAV. For two hundred and fifty pounds the Best Team Name is… drumroll please…

The lights flicker and go out.

They all shriek/general consternation.

BOBBY. Oh shit, oh Jesus Christ.

FRAN. It's happening.

RAV. Not yet. Not yet, it's too soon.

KATHY. We knew it was coming.

RAV. No, it can't. It's not finished yet. The Quiz.

Lights flicker back on.

Right, okay, quickly.

Kathy, Fran, could you help me with this, please?

A whiteboard or chalkboard appears from somewhere.

KATHY. I wondered what this was for.

RAV. In the words of *Blue Peter*, it's something I prepared earlier. Why was Peter so blue? Cheer up, Peter.

Let's get the music on. Bobby? Track number twelve, please.

'From the End of the World' by Electric Light Orchestra Plays.

Right now everyone, I need you to look back at your answer sheets and give me the *first letter* of the *first answer* in each round. Yeah?

Yeah?

KATHY. Slow down.

RAV. The *first letter* of the *first answer* in each round.

Read them out to me –

As they do he writes the first letter of each answer on the board vertically.

Round One. According to ABBA – where – Napoleon did surrender?

Waterloo.

Round Two. Which British city hosted the 1970 Commonwealth Games?

Edinburgh.

Round Three. Which was the first flag?

Wales.

Round Four. Who sang the theme tune for the TV series *One Foot in the Grave*?

Eric Idle.

Round Five. What do the millions of tiny rocks circling some planets' equators look like?

Rings.

Okay great. That's great.

And now the first letter of the last answer in each round.

Got it?

The first letter of the last answer in each round.

You've got it.

Okay, go.

Round One. Tracey who is the British artist who created 'Everyone I Have Ever Slept With 1963–1995'?

Emin.

Round Two. Discus and which other track and field event require safety netting? Hammer.

Round Three. The flag was Ecuador.

Round Four. Who directed *Alien*? Ridley Scott.

Round Five. Which planet…? Earth.

Okay, and looking at the board – what does that give us?

'W

E

W

E

R

E

H

E

R

E'

'WE WERE HERE'.

We were here.

KATHY. Oh, Rav.

RAV. And we were.

No matter what we've done or haven't done, what we've said or haven't, what we've got or what we've lost, no one can take that away from us.

We were here.

Say it with me – We were here. We were here. We were here.

The lights go out. They all huddle together.

BOBBY. This is it.

FRAN. Oh God.

RAV. I'm ready.

KATHY. Good luck, everyone.

The End (of the world).

The Last Quiz Night On Earth – Questions and Answers

Round One. General Knowledge

Q1. According to ABBA, my my, at – *where* – Napoleon did surrender?

A1. Waterloo

Q2: Which sign of the zodiac is represented by a lion?

A2. Leo

Q3. Who did Barack Obama defeat to win the 2012 US Presidential election?

A3. Mitt Romney

Q4. Globophobia is a fear of what?

A4. Balloons

Q5. In which decade was the first mobile-phone call made?

A5. 1970s

Q6. 'Everyone I Have Ever Slept With 1963–1995' is a work by British artist Tracey who?

A6. Emin

Round Two. Sport

Q1. Which British city hosted the 1970 Commonwealth Games?

A1. Edinburgh

Q2. Who was the first woman to beat a man at the PDC Darts World Championship?

A2. Fallon Sherrock

Q3. What is the heaviest weight category in boxing?

A3. Super heavyweight

Q4. Which is bigger, a full-sized football or a full-sized volleyball?

A5. A football

Q5. Who defeated Roger Federer to win a gold medal at the 2012 Olympic men's single final at Wimbledon?

A5. Andy Murray

Q6. Two throwing events in track and field require safety netting. Discus and what else?

A6: Hammer

Round Three. Flags

A1. Wales

A2. Switzerland

A3. Bosnia and Herzegovina

A4. China

A5. Bahamas

A6. Ecuador

Round Four. Film and Television

Q1. Which member of Monty Python sang the theme tune for the TV series *One Foot In The Grave*?

A1. Eric Idle

Q2. What was the first name of the character played by Kylie Minogue in *Neighbours*?

A2. Charlene

Q3. James Corden and Ruth Jones wrote which BBC comedy series that returned this Christmas for a special episode?

A3. *Gavin and Stacey*

Q4. Who played Dracula in the 1931 film of the same name?

A4. Bela Lugosi

Q5. Who voiced the forgetful blue tang fish in *Finding Nemo* and *Finding Dory*?

A5. Ellen DeGeneres

Q6. Who directed the film *Alien*?

A6. **R**idley Scott

Round Five. Space

Q1. Some planets have millions of tiny rocks circling their equator which look like – what?

A1. **R**ings

Q2. What is the name of the first satellite sent into space?

A2. Sputnik

Q3. Ganymede is a moon of which planet?

A3. Jupiter

Q4. Which is the coldest planet in the solar system?

A4. Neptune

Q5. The first woman in space Valentina Tereshkova is from which country?

A5. Russia

Q6. Which planet in our solar system is the only one not to be named after a Greek or Roman deity and – extra clue – is about to be hit by a life-ending asteroid?

A6. **E**arth

A Nick Hern Book

The Last Quiz Night on Earth first published in Great Britain as a paperback original in 2020 by Nick Hern Books Limited, The Glasshouse, 49a Goldhawk Road, London W12 8QP, in association with Box of Tricks Theatre Company

The Last Quiz Night on Earth copyright © 2020 Alison Carr

Alison Carr has asserted her right to be identified as the author of this work

Cover image: Sean Longmore, Quay Design

Designed and typeset by Nick Hern Books, London
Printed in the UK by Mimeo Ltd, Huntingdon, Cambridgeshire PE29 6XX

A CIP catalogue record for this book is available from the British Library

ISBN 978 1 84842 956 7

Woodland
CARBON
www.woodlandcarbon.co.uk
NICK HERN BOOKS
Printed on Carbon Captured paper

www.nickhernbooks.co.uk

facebook.com/nickhernbooks

twitter.com/nickhernbooks